Cedar Homes

Ideas for Log & Timber Frame Designs

Schiffer Publishing Ltd ®

4880 Lower Valley Road, Atglen, PA 19310 USA

Tina Skinner
Photography by Roger Wade

Published by Schiffer Publishing Ltd.
4880 Lower Valley Road
Atglen, PA 19310
Phone: (610) 593-1777; Fax: (610) 593-2002
E-mail: info@schifferbooks.com

We are always looking for people to write books on new and related subjects. If you have an idea
for a book please contact us at the above address.

This book may be purchased from the publisher.
Include $3.95 for shipping.
Please try your bookstore first.
You may write for a free catalog or visit www.schifferbooks.com

In Europe, Schiffer books are distributed by
Bushwood Books
6 Marksbury Ave.
Kew Gardens
Surrey TW9 4JF England
Phone: 44 (0) 20 8392-8585; Fax: 44 (0) 20 8392-9876
E-mail: Bushwd@aol.com
Free postage in the U.K., Europe; air mail at cost.

Library of Congress Cataloging-in-Publication Data

Skinner, Tina
Cedar homes ; ideas for log & timber frame designs / by Tina Skinner; photography by Roger
Wade.
p. cm.
ISBN 0-7643-1874-8 (hardcover)
1. Wooden-frame buildings. 2. Log buildings. 3. Architecture, Domestic.
I. Title.
NA4110.S54 2004
728'.37--dc21
2003008372

Designed by Tina Skinner
Type set in Garamond/Franklin Gothic

ISBN: 0-7643-1874-8
Printed in China

Foreword

Welcome! Town & Country is pleased to share with you our award winning white cedar homes in this exclusive collection. Strong, insulating and durable, Northern White Cedar is a wood that exudes warmth and evokes a unique charm second to none. Such are the homes that fill these pages. Designed with vision and built with integrity, you will find some of the best representations of log and timber frame homes created in the world within this sourcebook.

Northern White Cedar: a gift given from Mother Nature to a craftsman's skilled hands and on to a homeowner to live in and share with family for generations to come. The distinguishing features of Northern White Cedar include a unique cellular structure which make it resistant to rot, insects and decay. It has consistent light coloring and, much like a cork, will not absorb moisture.

At Town & Country, we've been crafting exceptional homes for more than half a century using only the heart of white cedar. This inner tree core is highly prized by wood artisans, viewed as the most exquisite and durable of natural woods. We pride ourselves on kiln-drying our logs, which are hand hewn in our own sawmill. All of our White Cedar is harvested in an environmentally sensitive manner from our timber strands in the Upper Peninsula of Michigan and Canada. Town & Country homes boast dramatic cathedral roof systems and soaring ceilings without sacrificing the warmth and coziness a home should possess. The comfort of any home is of vital importance and our homes are among the most energy efficient, well-insulated homes built today.

We invite you to linger over the images, ideas and inspirations we share in these pages. We hope this sourcebook will inspire you and expand your design horizons to guide you toward a home that serves as an individual expression that perfectly suits your tastes and lifestyle. Once you are ready to begin designing your log or timber frame home call us at 1.800.968.3178 or visit us on the web at www.cedarhomes.com.

Craig A. Andrews
President of Town & Country

Town & Country
Cedar Homes
Luxury built For Generations to Come...

Contents

Introduction

Like so many projects, this one grew out of others, a result of fortuitous contacts and mutual goals.

I'd been trying for many months to talk Roger Wade, an extraordinarily talented and prolific architectural photographer, and his wife, Debra Grahl, who is his stylist for photo shoots, into compiling their portfolio into a book. They'd been far too busy taking pictures. Yet while working, they spoke with a businessman who needed a way to showcase his beautiful homes.

Thus it came to this, a beautiful and inspiring book. It fell to me to get it organized and written. My fourth book on the subject, I worried that the Muse would desert me. However, once immersed in the images, I was quickly overcome by the same excitement I experience whenever I look at gorgeous homes.

I also heard the voice of a new muse: Stephen Biggs, the aforementioned businessman and chairman of the board at Town & Country Cedar Homes, left a lasting impression with me following our initial conversation. His message was that homebuyers who are making what is more than likely the biggest financial decision of their lives, are not necessarily using their heads, they're using their hearts. Looking at homes, contemplating living in them, is an emotional experience.

Of course, Mr. Biggs was citing market studies and industry analysis, and describing me. I look at these pictures like anyone else – dreaming of someday and somehow. Like you, I am looking for ideas I can incorporate into my home today,

and plans I can implement in my big, final dream project.

I find these images very stimulating. Log and timber frame homes strike a deep chord in the American conscience. They hark back to tradition and antiquity in the most material way. The construction methods shown are those that colonists and pioneers put to work when they settled this nation. And the structures we build this way today will very likely still stand for those who follow three hundred years hence.

Wood imparts a special beauty to a home. In this case we enjoy the honeyed tones of cedar, often left in the same shape nature grew it, straight and true trunks that buoy roofs; natural limbs and twigs that are incorporated as trim and decoration; even root bulbs put to work in unique designs.

The homes pictured here vary in outward style from contemporary to Colonial, shingle style to neo-classical. They range from rambling ranchers to colossal complexes to humble cabins. What they all have in common, however, is the inherent beauty of wood. This book is a celebration of the craftsmen and designers who work with trees, every ounce of their precious wood, to create homes that imbue pride in ownership.

All of the homes shown represent someone's dream come true. Each is a custom-built creation, specified to the homebuyer's lifestyle and needs. Each represents the fruition of months, even years, of planning.

This book is filled with ideas for your dream home.

– Tina Skinner

5

The Dream

Who doesn't imagine themselves here? Isolated in a rural retreat, surrounded by great vistas, be they snow-capped mountains or foam-capped waves. Nested in a warm home of our own creation, furnished for comfort and saturated in our individual sense of style.

Here is a home to live for. A retirement benefit to plan for. A vacation dream. Proudly nestled amidst rolling hills, sheltered on four sides by great overhanging eaves, and snugged in by enormous timbers.

This home announces rugged individual with refinement. A wood exterior is accented indoors by plaster finish and wood frame accents. The interior spirals around a central staircase, with the primary living areas focused toward a big, wrap-around deck and the vistas beyond.

The masters of the house enjoy exclusive use of the second floor, while two guest rooms downstairs allow them to entertain friends and loved ones.

FIRST FLOOR

SECOND FLOOR

8

Wooden outlines define this inspiring space, a living room that dominates an entire corner of the home. The bead-board ceiling and timbers were stained to match. Wood also creates tiers within a natural stone fireplace surround, where the mantel display of dried plants is mirrored in a lampshade and the natural forms used throughout the decor. Likewise, the tile flooring and case-iron accents are in keeping with the Craftsman era feeling of the home. An enormous expanse of white rises above the fireplace, creating the impression of sky within the room. Natural light floods the great room from two walls of windows and doors.

Dining room, kitchen, and living room are all open to each other in this home, and each enjoys a view out picture windows. Unpretentious furnishings were chosen for the dining set, eschewing formality. A wrought iron chandelier creates a cozy candlelight theme for diners. The bronze horse adds motion and excitement to the setting, flanked by zebra-striped lampshades. The sheerest of shades are set on the windows to tame the light on overwhelming days.

An arts and crafts style cabinet face was chosen for the kitchen, but in the subtlest of tones, stained to match the woodwork throughout the house. Glazed tiles add color and interest to the subtle, subdued space. In furnishing the kitchen with appliances, the owners found both black and white worked beautifully, keying in with wrought-iron furnishings and the plaster wall finishes. Island seating is the most popular for daily meals, and a popular place to perch before and after.

9

The working corner of the kitchen is dominated by double sinks, flanked by big windows. A dishwasher is conveniently located just to the right, allowing quick rinse and deposit action after the meal. Beyond, a deck beckons dining *al fresco*, weather permitting. The master bedroom is located on the second floor, under soaring ceilings. The same color theme is carried throughout the home: natural wood,

white walls, and subtle red accents. Wrought iron birds perch on the custom bed frame, in keeping with other iron accents throughout the home. Likewise, twin wrought iron beds fill one guest room and their semi-circle headboards are copied in wood in the other guest room. No room in the home was shorted on views, and heavy timber frames were used to accent the expansive picture windows.

Nature's Comforts

A home is an emotional well. We draw on it for our most basic needs -- sustenance, shelter, and a sense of security. It also houses our dearest memories of childhood and children, romantic moments, and emotional losses. For this reason, wood makes the most endearing vessel for our lives. Drawn from nature, timbers and boards bring their own histories to the home. Wood tones surround us in warmth, and offer a connection to our roots. This home marries the basic structure of log with classic style. The columned and arched portico recalls the grandeur and proportions of Greek architecture, while the materials keep it earthy. On closer inspection, one finds that those doric columns were fashioned by Nature herself. Slate-colored shingles are the perfect crown for this idealized woodland home. But don't be deceived by the simplistic appearance, inside the home unfolds in magnificent proportion.

The approach to this house suggests a ranch home, with a wonderful eave-sheltered entry porch and dormers for architectural interest. In the back, however, the home unfolds in three splendid stories, from a walkout basement where family and exercise rooms feed to a covered deck complete with a hot tub. A great room dominates the first floor, where the kitchen and dining areas open to the enormous deck. A two-story wall of windows floods the first and second floors with light.

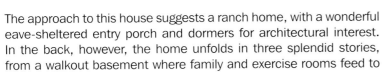

LOWER LEVEL   FIRST FLOOR   SECOND FLOOR

13

An enormous great room is the epicenter of the home, in the middle of the house, in the middle floor, in the midst of all the action. A central fireplace radiates warmth throughout the room, and up to the loft. Here a tranquil reading room and home office are one degree removed from the action to facilitate concentration. The open space is dominated by massive logs that support the cathedral ceiling and frame picture windows. In counterpoint, large river stones add mass at eye level, capped by a hand-hewn mantel. The bulk of the fireplace surround grounds the room for those seated in the comfortable arrangement of colorful furnishings. Note the natural branch balusters on the balcony, in contrast to finished straight rails in the border and around the staircase.

Dark green creates magic, making the walls almost disappear while showcasing the knotty pine cabinetry in the kitchen. Dark tones are reintroduced in the appliances, along with red highlights in the lighted sideboard cabinets and accent tiles. Stools were provided for informal seating at the island and a raised counter. Plus, a padded bench was snuggled under the window, with pillows to encourage guests to linger and keep the cook company. In the more formal dining room, the emphasis is on the views, both of the woods beyond, and of the great room adjacent. A transom of custom stained glass window filters light above the sideboard. Finished logs were left exposed, revealing the structural bones of the home, and offering an easy conversational icebreaker for first-time guests. Candles, crystal, and finely crafted furnishings add a formal touch to the casual homespun placemats and shaded chandelier.

17

Outdoor pleasures weren't neglected in this sprawling homestead. A sunken hot spa seems to spring naturally from a rock patio. Nearby, a pavilion supported by whole tree trunks spreads its limbs for outdoor gatherings lit by an antler chandelier and a stone fireplace.

Matching barstools and dining chairs unite kitchen and dining areas, but there is a definite formal divide, as well. A sculpted carpet and drapes add elegance to the dining room, creating a space acceptable for entertaining, though as easily adapted to everyday family dinners. A bow window floods both rooms with light, aided on cloudy days by recessed spotlights in the wood ceiling. A baker's paradise, the kitchen was equipped with impressive expanses of countertop.

Left: Wood is emphasized in an impressive entry foyer, where one passes between mullioned sidelights and under a massive transom where solid logs frame triangular transoms. Beyond the foyer sits the home's focal great room, where comfortable, semi-formal leather furnishings are arranged amidst pillars of natural finish cedar logs.

Cabin Fever

For so many, this is the dream. To simplify things, if only for a week or two, to live quietly, in a small place, in a tree-shaded glen. Close to nature. Part of nature. Wood walls put you at one with the surrounding trees, maximum windows put you in the forest, though sheltered from its elements. A fire burns within. Plus, a hot tub bubbles and steams just outside. After all, this isn't some shoddy prehistoric fantasy!

FIRST FLOOR

STOR.
5/6 X 3/0

1/2 BATH
5/6 X 5/3

KITCHEN
11/0 X 10/0

PORCH

DN

UP

DINING
9/4 X 12/5

LIVING
15/6 X 17/1

DECK AREA
26/0 X 10/0

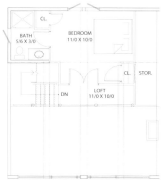

SECOND FLOOR

CL.

BATH
5/6 X 3/0

BEDROOM
11/0 X 10/0

CL.   STOR.

DN

LOFT
11/0 X 10/0

41

An open floor plan puts kitchen, dining, and living areas in close contact. All benefit from the light from an open wall of windows, and the fire that burns in a wonderful stone fireplace. Log construction was carried indoors, to frame an eating counter in the kitchen, and to support a sleeping loft above. A clever basket weaver created the faux moose head overlooking the scene.

43

44

Wood tones and skin tones, so similar and warm. Rising from a Berber carpet, a staircase is composed of an entire tree trunk for support, half timber steps, and handpicked branches for rails and balusters. The walls are exposed logs, the ceiling stained-to-match bead board. And as a centerpiece, a custom crafted dinette set of bent willow.

Green trim in the window moldings and gutter system add a complementary outline to the structure. In the front, dormer windows were used to add architectural interest and, in the case of the window on the left, to feed light to a second-floor bath.

51

The central living area of the home is awesome in its proportions. The massive timbers that define the cathedral ceiling and support it are works of wonder. The interior decor seems to hardly matter in comparison. So in furnishing the great room, dining room, and kitchen, the owners drew further from Nature. Leather seating and vegetal-dye textiles dominate the living area. In the kitchen, a stone hood caps the cooktop. The dining room features a highly lacquered picnic table cut straight from the woods. Throughout, animal forms add ornament.

It is rare that a home plan allows a kitchen to have such a raised ceiling. Taking advantage of the height, the stone fireplace climbs to the rafters. This home is endowed with unique touches

throughout. For example, this powder room sink, cut from a boulder, and the tree system that supports it. In the loft, an arched doorway opens to a small home office area under the eaves.

Mountain Majesty

Creating a mountain home presents topographical challenges to the designer, but none that can't be overcome. Here, reinforced stone pillars shore up a great octagonal porch, which presents itself as a castle tower and appeals to our deepest yearning for fairytale homes. The result is a home that opens in back to the forest, with three stories of access to the outdoors. Should that prove daunting to any guests, or the home's owners as they age, an elevator was installed to ease the transit of occupants or their picnics.

LOWER LEVEL

STORAGE

MECH ROOM

LOW VOLTAGE ROOM

REC. ROOM
23/8x37/1

HOT TUB ROOM
16/6x15/3

DRESSING ROOM

DRESSING ROOM

BATH
6/5x6/8

STORAGE

FIRST FLOOR

NOOK
13/4x13/7

GREAT ROOM

KITCHEN
15/7x17/9

24/11x24/11

M. BEDROOM
15/6x24/6

M. BATH
17/9x15/3

M. CLOSET
15/3x13/7

LINDA'S ROOM
18/6x11/1

STORAGE
9/0x10/0

BATH
9/1x5/5

HALL

UP

DINING ROOM
18/3x13/1

ENTRY
8/1x13/1

COVERED PORCH

JOHN'S ROOM
13/6x19/11

HOBBY RM.
21/1x11/1

SECOND FLOOR

STORAGE

BATH
7/1x10/11

BEDROOM
13/7x15/6

REC. ROOM
11/1x15/9

BEDROOM
14/2x14/2

HALL

BATH

BATH
9/8x10/11

BEDROOM
14/2x14/3

75

Bronze geese consider the landing in front of this beautiful
entryway. The home has been elegantly landscaped with
rocks, shrubs, and ornamental grasses in a successful
attempt to restore what construction uprooted. Their love of
nature led the owners to log home construction.

Decks, patios, porches, and sunrooms — this home was built to accommodate outdoors lovers. Note the sandbox just outside the screened porch, a perfect place to send tots where you can keep an eye on them. Tempered glass takes the place of wood ballusters, freeing the view through the deck railing.

A varied roofline on the exterior makes for a spectacular ceiling inside. Ceiling heights help to define spaces within the open floor plan of the living areas. Here the great room, dining area, and kitchen share a common floor, but the landscape changes drastically above. A light finish on the wood walls and ceiling adds to the airy feeling of the space, while dark furnishings in the living room ground and center the occupants.

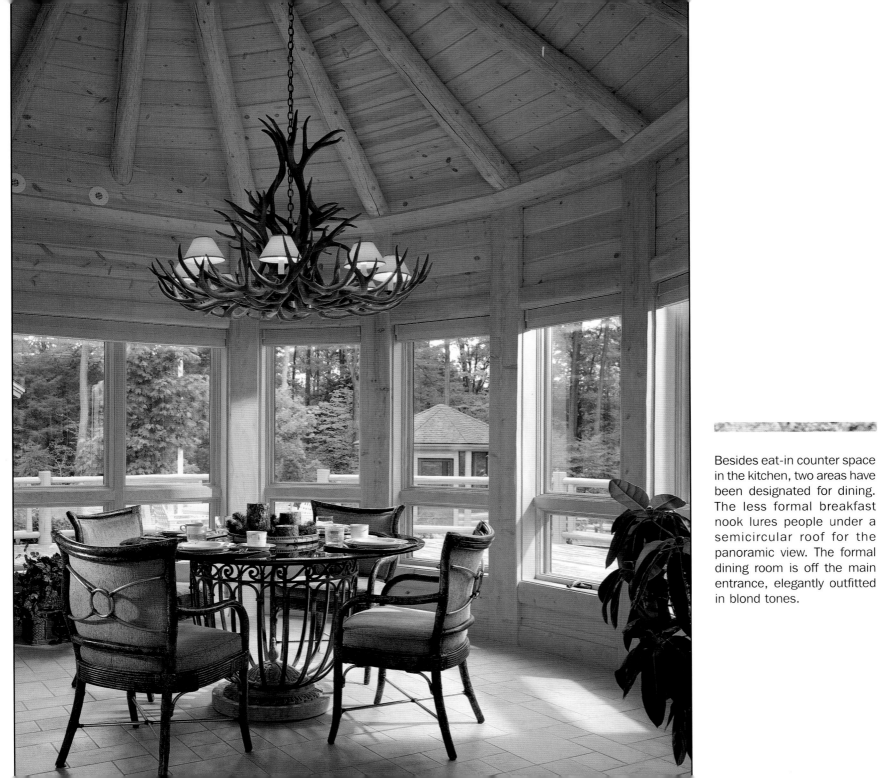

Besides eat-in counter space in the kitchen, two areas have been designated for dining. The less formal breakfast nook lures people under a semicircular roof for the panoramic view. The formal dining room is off the main entrance, elegantly outfitted in blond tones.

81

The master bed and bath suite were located on the first floor, in plans for retirement. Plus, the boys were old enough that the parents were happy to see them tucked in on the second floor, out of earshot. Canoe ornaments tub-side are inspiration for outings on the larger body of water beyond, a small lake.

93

Tudor Revival

When British craftsmen created this picturesque style during the reign of the Tudor monarchs, it was done as a simple means to an end. Tree trunks or great logs were erected in the shape of the letter A and the gaps filled in with some form of mortar, the result being stripes that revealed the home's structure. The form was perfected and elaborated upon, and soon outgrew its structural origins to become a form of decoration. Moreover, as the style developed, it became standard to attach half timbers to stucco, creating the look while saving on materials. Here is a home where the owners elected to go whole log. The result is a glorious home, set atop a rugged stone foundation.

FIRST FLOOR

DECK
13/7 X 76/0

DINING
16/0 X 16/7

GREAT ROOM
21/3 X 21/0

MASTER BEDROOM
15/6 X 16/4

KITCHEN
15/6 X 15/1

W.I.C.
3/8/6 J.

LINEN

MASTER BATH
15/6 X 13/8

LAUNDRY
9/8 X 5/6

PANTRY

DN

STAIRS

POWDER
ROOM
0/0 X 8/0

ENTRY
6/6 X 15/7

W.I.C.
7/6 X 7/7

D   W

COVERED
PORCH
26/0 X 6/0

SECOND FLOOR

GAME/BUNK ROOM
21/1 X 20/10

BEDROOM #2
15/0 X 16/0

BEDROOM #3
15/0 X 16/0

W.I.C.

HALL
21/1 X 5/6

BATH #2
9/3 X 8/1

BATH #1
5/1 X 12/0

LAV.#2

LINEN

CL.

CL.

UP

SKI ROOM
15/1 X 8/0

MECH
8/1 X 14/5

GARAGE
20/0 X 17/11

CL.

95

The great room stretches the width of the building. The home's log trusses were left open above. The informal space encompasses room for one of the master's passions – billiards. The room's centerpiece, a stone chimney, was masterfully crafted from a mixture of rocks in various sizes, making it appear to be something Nature herself designed.

Leather seating stretches along a granite countertop, the defining line for an open kitchen. Adjacent, a dining area opens to magnificent views.

A handsomely appointed master bedroom suite was located on the first floor. Above, each of two children was given a bedroom on either side of a game and bunkroom, with full baths for each.

101

Family Style

Architecturally interesting from any angle, this home was packed with roof peaks, bowed extensions, recessed porches, and a fantastic semi-circular stone room that is home to the household kitchen. The children were tucked neatly side-by-side in upstairs bedrooms, each with a dormer window of their own, and a loft area where toys and children's games rule. Downstairs, the parents enjoy a spacious master suite. A great room occupies one wing of the house, top to bottom. This lofty gathering place opens to an expansive deck that wraps around to the front entry porch. On the other side, a garage creates a rear family entrance. Separating the kitchen and dining areas and the great room is unusual in today's house designs, but the overall effect of the home is one that artfully divides public areas from more private family quarters.

FIRST FLOOR

KITCHEN
15/7 X 12/7

M. BATH
8/2 X 12/6

MASTER
BEDROOM
14/6 X 19/8

STOR

GARAGE
21/1 X 25/10

WALK-IN
CLOSET
8/4 X 6/8

DINING ROOM
15/3 X 12/1

CL

CL.

STO

LIN

BATH
7/8 X
7/9

DEN
10/5 X 14/6

UTIL/LAUN
12/5 X 8/4

D

W

ENTRY
6/6 X 17/0

CLO

GREAT ROOM
30/11 X 24/7

SECOND FLOOR

OPEN TO BELOW

BEDROOM #2
11/6 X 14/10

BEDROOM #3
11/6 X 14/10

BEDROOM #4
11/7 X 21/4

CL.

CL.

VANITY
3/0 X 7/7

BATH
6/6 X 7/9

LOFT AREA
17/1 X 21/11

OPEN TO BELOW

A wooden porch ushers visitors right into the heart of a warm family home. Besides the entry foyer, the porch offers access to the family deck areas that wrap around the great room where family members gather. Workers carefully built around existing trees, allowing the family the advantage of mature foliage to shade the outdoor sitting areas.

103

Hunting trophies and a classic moped prove dad played a hand in decorating the great room. The home's architectural details include an expanse of railing crafted from tree branches. The fireplace forms the center of attention – two stories of river stone rising to the top of the cathedral ceiling. Electronic entertainments were neatly tucked into custom cabinetry set under the stairs. Native American themes predominate in the dining area. The circular stone wall provides for a unique kitchen configuration, and a wondrous, wagon wheel ceiling.

LOWER LEVEL

BEDROOM
15/4 X 15/4

REC. ROOM
25/1 X 23/1

STORAGE
15/4 X 17/5

BATH
10/8 X 8/0

UP

BASEMENT
34/10 X 12/8

MECH.
15/4 X 6/5

BATH
6/8 X
8/5

STAIRS

UP

FIRST FLOOR

DECK AREA

DECK AREA

MASTER BEDROOM
15/6 X 16/6

GREAT ROOM
24/3 X 23/5

DINING
15/6 X 13/11

SCREENED PORCH

M.BATH
105 SQ. FT.

W.I. CLOSET

1/2
BATH

FOYER
9/1 X 13/4

U

PANTRY
7/8 X
5/6

KITCHEN
15/7 X 17/11

LNDRY

REAR ENTRY

U

BATH
7/6 X
5/8

MECH.
9/4 X 5/9

COVERED
PORCH

GARAGE
31/1 X 29/3

SECOND FLOOR

BEDROOM #3
15/3 X 15/6

CL

OPEN TO BELOW

BEDROOM #4
15/6 X 18/2

CATWALK
23/1 X 5/2

D

CL

BATH
11/3 X 5/10

BEDROOM #2
15/3 X 12/11

CL

BATH
12/6 X 5/9

OPEN TO BELOW

D
STAIR

117

REC. ROOM
29/1 X 24/0

BATH
9/1 X 6/7

CL

CL

The irregular round river stones in the foundation and chimney add wonderful contrast to the straight and sturdy log home. Glass is another contrasting element in the handsome facade, with its sleek face and a minimal use of mullioned panes.

The lake is a draw both day and night, so lighting adds not only art, but safety to stairs on the deck. A three-bay garage is nice for the cars, but the family members particularly enjoy the rec room above. It's the perfect removed spot for those who want to stay up into the wee hours while others are trying to rest.

Opposite page: The great room is the primary gathering spot in this vacation home. The family enjoys playing cards, board games, and putting puzzles together, so a table with padded chairs was the obvious choice for the choicest view the house had to offer. Tree trunks flank the fireplace, showcasing nature's art beside a sparingly adorned mantel. Left: A wet bar is a featured attraction on the screened porch.

121

A burgundy finish breaks up the effect of wood and white wall in the kitchen. In the dining room, a custom-made table celebrates the trees.

Opposite page: An arched wood door adds charm to an entryway. The foyer is also home to one of two staircases that access the second floor. The first flight to the landing is composed of half-round logs, a pleasing touch to the log décor. Likewise, the entry is personalized with a canoe-themed area rug, reflecting a favorite pastime on the lake beyond. Above: Master bed and bath were painted royal blue, a soothing color that complements the lake view.

Retirement Plan

That favorite lake where your family first rented, then bought, then built. The goal: to always live those happy, carefree times, where you weren't rushed to race to work, to put away the groceries, to get dinner on the table. And so, in your master plan you include a home office. The kids move out, finish college. No more tuition. You scale back your needs, and then you take the plunge. It's heaven, just the way you planned it. Room for the kids when they want to come. A place the grandchildren will beg to visit.

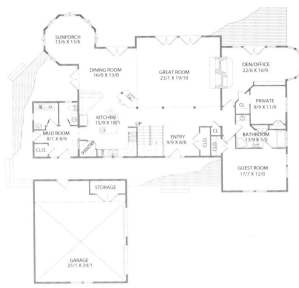

FIRST FLOOR

SUNPORCH
13/6 X 13/6

DINING ROOM
16/0 X 13/0

GREAT ROOM
23/1 X 19/10

DEN/OFFICE
22/6 X 10/9

PRIVATE
9/9 X 11/0

KITCHEN
15/9 X 18/1

UP

ENTRY
9/9 X 8/6

CL

BATHROOM
13/9 X 5/0

MUD ROOM
8/1 X 8/9

CLO.

PANTRY

CLO.

CL

GUEST ROOM
17/7 X 12/0

STORAGE

GARAGE
25/1 X 29/1

SECOND FLOOR

BEDROOM
15/7 X 15/2

OPEN TO
BELOW

MASTER BEDROOM
16/1 X 14/0

CLO.

CLO.

DN

MST. CLO.
9/9 X 7/9

BEDROOM
13/10 X 12/10

STORAGE
9/9 X 6/8

LOFT
15/9 X 13/10

LINEN

BATH
8/5 X 6/0

CLO.

MASTER BATH
14/4 X 14/6

BONUS ROOM
15/1 X 25/9

Twin jet skis sit poised for action. For the owners, a skim around the lake is akin to an afternoon walk on nearby trails, both ready for the asking on sunny afternoons.

127

A barn-style roofline and varied heights and cutouts add architectural interest to this home. Extensive decking reflects the family's penchant for being outdoors. After all, the fresh country air and lakeside location were the initial attractions.

The master bedroom occupies a wing on the first floor, while guest bedrooms are upstairs and in the basement. Lots of accommodations have been provided for holiday time and weekend gatherings throughout the year. When the house is empty and quiet, a loft reading area is a favorite hangout for the lady of the house.

143

Pastoral Palace

Set in a very private meadow, there was no need to design a grand entry. In fact, this home enjoys private porches, decks, and patios all the way around. Though a foyer was forsaken, there's not a room in the home that wouldn't impress. Rather, the family focused on living in their home when they designed it. They enter through the three-car garage, and take any number of exits when they want to partake of the fresh air and views.

DECK
22/0 X 14/4

COVERED PORCH
12/0 X 6/0

MASTER
BEDROOM
17/1 X 29/1

M. BATHROOM
12/0 X 9/10

W/I CLOSET
12/0 X 7/6

GREAT ROOM
21/1 X 21/2

UP

DWN

COVERED PORCH
24/0 X 6/0

1/2 BATH
5/0 X 5/10

PANTRY
7/3 X 7/11

CLO

CLO

GARAGE
21/1 X 39/1

KITCHEN
15/7 X 13/9

W
D

CLO

UTIL/LAUN
5/2 X 10/7

COVERED PORCH
29/8 X 6/0

DINING ROOM
21/1 X 13/11

COVERED PORCH
24/0 X 6/0

FIRST FLOOR

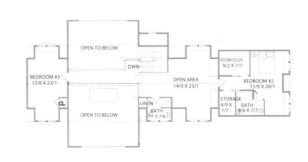

OPEN TO BELOW

BEDROOM #3
12/0 X 23/1

OPEN TO BELOW

DWN

LINEN

BATH
7/1 X 7/0

OPEN AREA
14/0 X 23/1

STOR/CLOS
9/2 X 7/7

BEDROOM #2
11/8 X 20/1

STORAGE
4/9 X
7/7

BATH
8/6 X 7/7

SECOND FLOOR

146

A kitchen was designed for utility, with handsome cabinets stacked for maximum storage, in addition to a spacious pantry. Stools provide seating adjacent to the work area, but the truly comfortable dining takes place right next door, where soft seating offers a place to linger by the fire and savor both food and family. White wallboard creates contrast with wooden supports and door frames, emphasizing a stunning arrangement of triangular windows over French doors.

Above: A catwalk and library loft overlook the great room and dining room areas below, while benefiting from the heat of the stone fireplace. Opposite page: The master bedroom occupies its own wing of the home, commanding a grand space under a cathedral ceiling. Besides acres of view, the bedroom opens to covered porches on both sides. A walk-in closet and master bath provide a sound buffer between the living areas and the owners' sleeping quarters.

Outside the Box

There's a wonderful sense of freedom in stepping free of the traditional square box home design and playing with new shapes and forms. Log certainly doesn't place limits on the design, as this home clearly demonstrates. Three octagonal areas were designed into the home, one on each rear corner, another in the center stairwell for a truly well rounded sense. The stairwell's projection adds a bow window to the second floor, while half-circle windows flank it on either side. The roofline is varied in back by a thrusting cathedral ceiling that supports a two-story picture window. The result is lots of light and unique living spaces within, plus a lovely horizon of roofline to look back on.

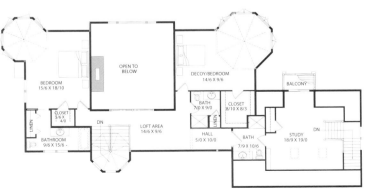

FIRST FLOOR

SITTING AREA
10/0 X 10/0

GREAT ROOM
20/0 X 21/0

DECK AREA

DINING ROOM
13/0 X 13/0

KING

MASTER BEDROOM
15/6 X 15/6

GARAGE
31/0 X 23/0

W/I CLOSET
11/9 X 7/0

KITCHEN
16/10 X 13/9

UP

W/C
3/9 X 6/0

M. BATHROOM
11/6 X 8/3

CLOSET

FOYER
9/9 X 8/3

BATH
5/6 X 5/9

CLOSET

STORAGE

PORCH

LAUNDRY
16/0 X 8/9

D   W

UP

SECOND FLOOR

BEDROOM
15/6 X 18/10

OPEN TO BELOW

DECOY/BEDROOM
14/6 X 9/6

BALCONY

LINEN

CLOSET
5/6 X 4/0

DN

LOFT AREA
14/6 X 9/6

BATH
7/0 X 9/0

CLOSET
8/10 X 8/3

LINEN

BATHROOM
9/6 X 15/6

HALL
5/0 X 10/0

BATH
7/9 X 10/6

STUDY
18/9 X 19/0

DN

151

A domed door reflects the arch of windows beyond. From a fairly humble entry, underlined by slate tiles, the home opens to an spacious great room. Enormous boulders were stacked to surround the fireplace, the focal point by night in this beautiful home. By day, the window draws all eyes.

153

Colorful accents highlight the custom cabinetry that spans kitchen and dining areas. The result is a seamless expanse of woodwork, with a midline created by polished granite countertop. An adjacent log top bar serves guests.

Master bed and bath include a circular projection used as a sitting area, access to the back deck, and a whirlpool tub built for two.

Pooling Together

There are places you simply never want to leave, and that's best when you just happen to be at home! This lucky family enjoys a vacation getaway daily, complete with a full-size indoor pool. Dad even works at home, in a private office tucked away in the basement. Bedrooms are tucked into corners of the home, while the central areas are massive, open, and designed to draw family members together. The entryway is inviting, the home's name hanging from huge rafters in a drive-through portico that makes unloading the groceries a weather-proof task.

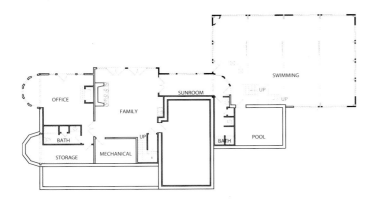

LOWER LEVEL

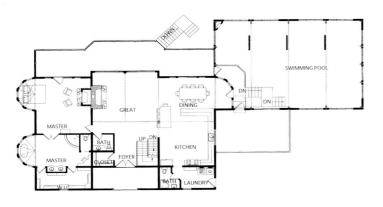

FIRST FLOOR

SECOND FLOOR

Season's greetings: a country collection of Santas, sleds, and greenery greets family members and guests in this handsome entryway, sheltered by massive timbers.

159

A great room (opposite page) dominates the center of the home. It is open to the roof, with an amazing, two-story wall of windows and a stone fireplace. The room is packed with comfy furniture that draws members close to the fire, and each other. For more private moments, mom and dad have reserved this crisp little sitting area fireside in the master bedroom.

Suspended see-through cabinets add storage while maintaining the open feeling with the dining room beyond. Arts and Crafts-style stained glass lamps add color to the central island workstation/buffet, as well as the more formal dining area beyond. A stone surround creates a hearth-like appeal for the professional cooktop and oven. The massive dining table seats ten, allowing plenty of room for frequent dinner guests.

A downstairs family room is a major draw. A wet bar, built-in media center, and proximity to the pool make this the most popular hangout. The male majority in the household is reflected in the choice of motifs for the custom carpeting. When not staying dry by the wet bar, the family members enjoy getting wet year round. The poolroom stays warm despite snow outside, and the heated waters are an excellent place to stay fit and free of the winter blahs.

166

The master bed and bath are situated by two semi-circular bay windows on the first floor. The result is a flood of light for the dreamers, be they in bed or the whirlpool tub. The eldest child was given a master suite on the second floor, complete with fireplace, walk-in-closet, and a private bath. When all the children have moved out, this will be their favorite place to stay on return visits.

167

Rural
Sprawl

A sheltered doorway beckons: a custom, hand-carved door is set in a stone surround and sheltered by a log-supported porch. Once through the doorway, one finds themself in an immense complex, with an option to turn left, right, or go straight ahead. Arranged within a triangular form, the home unfolds easily through kitchen and great room. For the family members, more intimate and practical spaces are located on either side of the central aisle, as well as above and below. Outside, the architectural profile is greatly varied by peaked roofs and bay window projections. A full basement has been only partially utilized as a fitness center, but holds great potential as the family's needs and hobbies grow.

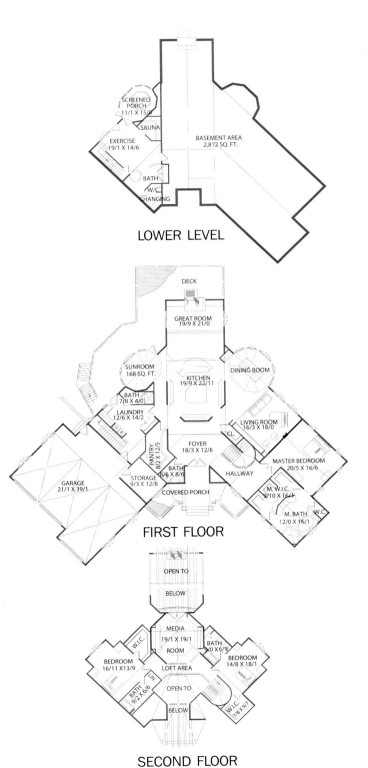

LOWER LEVEL

SCREENED PORCH
11/1 X 15/8

SAUNA

EXERCISE
19/1 X 14/6

BASEMENT AREA
2,812 SQ. FT.

BATH

W/C

CHANGING

FIRST FLOOR

DECK

GREAT ROOM
19/9 X 21/0

SUNROOM
168 SQ. FT.

KITCHEN
19/9 X 22/11

DINING ROOM

BATH
7/8 X 4/0

LAUNDRY
12/6 X 14/2

LIVING ROOM
16/3 X 18/0

PANTRY
8/2 X 12/5

FOYER
18/3 X 12/8

CL.

MASTER BEDROOM
20/5 X 16/6

GARAGE
21/1 X 39/1

BATH
8/6 X 8/6

STORAGE
9/3 X 12/8

HALLWAY

M. W.I.C.
9/10 X 16/4

COVERED PORCH

M. BATH
12/0 X 16/1

W/C

SECOND FLOOR

OPEN TO

BELOW

MEDIA
19/1 X 19/1

ROOM

BATH
9/0 X 6/9

W.I.C.

BEDROOM
16/11 X13/9

BEDROOM
14/8 X 18/1

LOFT AREA

BATH
9/2 X 6/6

LIN.

OPEN TO

BELOW

W.I.C.
17/8 X 9/7

Deck snuggles the back of the home, offering a private outdoor vantage within a nest of trees. Grey and beige stains add subtle variety to the wood exterior, helping it mesh with river stone foundation and chimney.

169

Log walls have been beaded to offer a unique, panel-like texture to the central living areas. Intact tree trunks support the cathedral ceiling in the great room, where the skyline is also made impressive with custom ironwork balusters along the loft and stair railings. The equestrian theme on the front door is carried through in the artwork.

171

Both dining areas – formal and sunroom/breakfast nook – are open to the other living areas, and defined primarily by their domed roofs.

The master bedroom is an impressive space made exotic by the rich furnishings and wood surfaces.

Soaking It All In

A second home by the lake is where this couple manages to wash away all cares and concerns. What kinks the hot tub can't work out, a good dose of sun on the dock can fade away. If forced inside, there's a sauna to do the soothing.

This compact little home is big on deck space outdoors, though spacious accommodations were provided inside for inclement weather. An artist, the owner included a studio with a lake view in the plan.

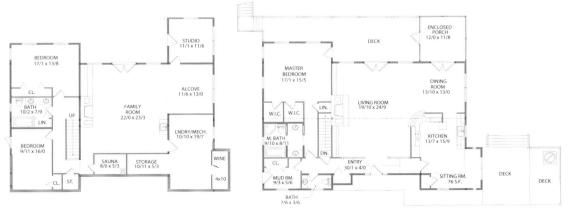

175

LOWER LEVEL

BEDROOM
17/1 x 13/8

CL.

BATH
10/2 x 7/9

LIN.

UP

BEDROOM
9/11 x 16/0

CL.

ST.

SAUNA
8/0 x 5/3

STORAGE
10/11 x 5/3

FAMILY
ROOM
22/0 x 23/3

STUDIO
11/1 x 11/6

ALCOVE
11/6 x 13/0

LNDRY/MECH.
10/10 x 19/7

WINE

4x10

FIRST FLOOR

MASTER
BEDROOM
17/1 x 15/5

W.I.C.

W.I.C.

LIN.

M. BATH
9/10 x 8/11

CL.

DN.

MUD RM.
9/3 x 5/6

BATH
7/6 x 3/6

DECK

LIVING ROOM
19/10 x 24/9

ENTRY
30/1 x 4/0

ENCLOSED
PORCH
12/0 x 11/8

DINING
ROOM
13/10 x 13/0

KITCHEN
13/7 x 15/9

SITTING RM.
76 S.F.

DECK

DECK

Two levels of lawn divided by a terraced hill stand between the homeowners and a speedboat. It's a journey they happily undertake several times a day during vacation weekends. Sticks create an artful front door and matching sidelights for this charming log cabin home.

A library of good reads is stacked up next to the stone fireplace. A mullioned transom over the entryway feeds light into the family room while preserving the family's privacy. The home is adorned with original artwork that was fashioned from wood, stone, and other lightly modified natural materials. A crescent shaped window adds architectural interest to the back of the home, light to the interior.

The master bedroom, like the rest of the house, was furnished by Nature, slightly modified. A birch-bark mirror and "twig" built bed are in keeping with the log cabin environment. The sun porch furnishings were upholstered in reproduction barkcloth, which adds tropical flair.

The owner displays a collection of basketry between kitchen and dining areas. Here, as throughout the home, her penchant for rustic furnishings is evident.

A guest room is tucked under the
eaves, lit by the triangular windows
that characterize this home.

205

Great Escape

The getaway: secluded in the mountains, sheltered by trees. Snowed in for what you wish would be weeks. There are two kinds of people – those who head for the sea-shore, and those who head to the hills. For the hill folk, a log cabin is the ideal camping ground. There's a big fire roaring inside, comfy chairs arranged around it. The larder is stocked with canned goods, and you're good to go. So bring on the snow!

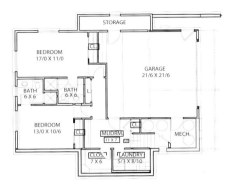

LOWER LEVEL

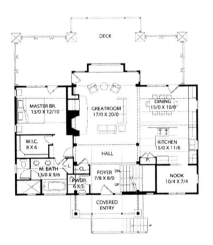

FIRST FLOOR

SECOND FLOOR

A roaring fire is the first prerequisite for a weekend cabin in winter. While waiting for the thaw, a fishing rod works as minimalist adornment above the enormous picture window. An open living/kitchen/dining room works beautifully in a cabin where people get away to be together.

Lights set within a grid add Oriental flair to the ceiling and work with the minimalist décor. Padded chairs and big windowpanes encourage diners to linger at the dining table, though a nearby nook is a great place to grab a quick bite on stools.

Okay, so you can never truly get away from it all. Still, the little business details, the phone calls that have to be made, paperwork to be filled out, can be isolated on the second floor.

Two guest rooms are located in the basement, with private baths. The master suite (shown) is on the first floor. The owners kept the dimensions modest as they spend more time in other areas of the home.

Reflecting on Beauty

Talk about a big first impression – an arch of solid wood greets visitors who pull up the circular drive to this enormous portico. Symmetrical design in matching bow windows topped by arched openings add to the initial appeal of this fantastic residence. Inside is a fascinating study in family planning. The children have their own wing over the garage, with two powder rooms, a shared bath, and a game loft. Spanning both first and second floors, the master suite opens to a private study and exercise room above. Between the two is an enormous expanse of family space, open two-stories high. The central living complex is divided between the more formal guest areas – foyer and living room – on one side, the family room and eating areas on the other. Located on a hefty parcel of land, the owners allowed room in the garage for golf carts – the fastest way to the nearby lake.

215

FIRST FLOOR

DECK
1,150 SQ. FT.

NOOK

FAMILY RM

DOUBLE
FIREPLACE

LIVING RM

MASTER SUITE

CL.

KITCHEN

UP

CL.

CL.

UP

FOYER

CL.

UP

MST BATH

MECH

LNDRY

DINING

GOLF CARTS

PORCH
23/0 X 10/0

GARAGE

SECOND FLOOR

OPEN TO
BELOW

OPEN TO
BELOW

GAME LOFT
11/0 X 16/3

OPEN TO
BELOW

STUDY
17/1 X 8/1

BALCONY
17/3 X 4/7

DN.

BEDROOM
11/9 X 14/3

CL.

DN.

EXERCISE ROOM
17/1 X 11/7

BEDROOM
11/9 X 14/3

STORAGE
9/10 X 7/0

OPEN TO
BELOW

CL.

VANITY
7/0 X 7/0

BATH

BEDROOM
9/10 X 17/9

VANITY
7/0 X 7/0

CL.

No part of a tree need be wasted, as this bridge made of roots demonstrates. This home was exquisitely landscaped, front and back, befitting its lakeside location.

217

Mimicking the front profile of the home, the rear façade features a central arch of window under a peaked roof. A manmade stream and small fish pond add interest to the landscape.

Connected by a see-through fireplace, a family room and living room sit side-by-side on the ground floor of the home. Both offer magnificent vistas.

Built-in seating in the kitchen provides a favorite family dining spot. The open plan allows several hands to undertake cooking tasks for the family or guests.

A staircase in the foyer leads to a balcony and the children's wing of the home.

222

The master suite is an estate unto itself. This view shows the walkway into the sleeping area. To the right is an enormous walk-in closet circling a spiral staircase that leads to the second floor of the suite – home to a study and exercise room.

Last Resort

Here's a home that harvests all the homeowners' many years of experience. Their retirement home, it represents all that they imagine needing. It was laid out according to how they live. And it is filled with all the favorite things they've accumulated in a lifetime. Work is now a hobby, and two home offices allow the couple the leisure to apply themselves to their curtailed careers as they please. Moreover, they double as guest rooms when the children want to visit. Most importantly, the home offers them vistas of a property they saved years to buy, far from the maddening crowd.

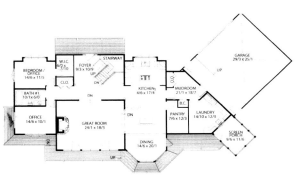

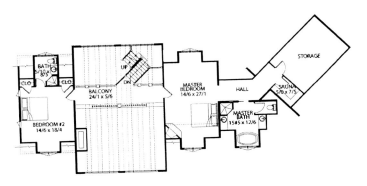

FIRST FLOOR

SECOND FLOOR

225

226

Relatively modest in proportion by today's new homes standards, these homebuilders didn't stint on a grand

entry. From the timbered porch, to the log and tile
foyer, the home makes a hefty first impression.

227

The great room was furnished for everyday use, with a coffee table the owners prop their feet up on, a fire and throw blankets to keep them toasty.

228